Australian Découpage

Australian Découpage

Vivienne Garforth

Kangaroo Press

Dedication

For Lindsay and Joyce

Acknowledgments

I would like to offer my appreciation to the following people and companies for so willingly giving me permission to use their products and for supplying me with samples.
• Pettis Studios in Melbourne for supplying their beautiful floral design paper products.
• Phil Taylor Studios of Sydney for permission to use their koala and wildflower paper.
• Card Sharp of Avalon in New South Wales for supplying samples of their papers, including the Barrier Reef fish, poinsettia and baby animals designs.
• Richard Galbraith of Evelyn Studios in Victoria for providing samples of his wonderful comic animal papers, including the koala ballerinas.
• Harper-Collins Publishing in Sydney for granting me permission to use the birds from *What Bird is That?* by Neville Cayley, first published in 1931 by Angus and Robertson.
• Goldfields-Esperance Travel Association in Kalgoorlie-Boulder in Western Australia for permission to use their travel brochure.
• Timber Turn Pty Ltd of Panorama, South Australia, for permission to use their wooden magazine holder, picture frame, tissue-box cover and circular box.
• Swanland Crafts in Perth for supplying the coloured cards and black bookmark blanks used in the paper-tole section.
• Robyn Lakeman from Aqua Unicorn Images Pty Ltd of Elwood in Victoria for supplying samples of their colourful stained glass birds and wildflowers découpage paper.
• Allan Cornwell for granting me permission to use the sepia pictures from the 1993 Angus and Robertson *Australian Heritage Diary*.
• Lindsay Muskett for once again using his skill and expertise with the camera to photograph all of the découpaged items in truly Australian settings, creating the image which I required—an Australian country feeling.

© Vivienne Garforth 1994

First published in 1994 by Kangaroo Press Pty Ltd
3 Whitehall Road Kenthurst NSW 2156 Australia
P.O. Box 6125 Dural Delivery Centre NSW 2158
Typeset by G.T. Setters Pty Limited
Printed in China through Colorcraft Ltd

ISBN 0 86417 580 9

Contents

Introduction   6
History of découpage   7
Materials   7
Sources of Australian paper motifs   10
Terracotta pots   12
Three tins with different finishes   15
Postage stamp desk set   19
Gum blossom wooden dressing table set   21
Barrier Reef brick doorstop   25
Billy kitchen tool container   27
Lampshade base and photo frame   29
Australian parrots placemats, coasters and napkin rings   31
Photo album cover   34
Papier-mâché boxes   37
Greeting cards and bookmarks   40
Christmas decorations   42
Kerosene lamp   45
Aussie mixture bookends   47
Doll's wardrobe and cot   49
Ballerina koalas box   51
Wooden magazine rack   55
Goldfields letterbox   56
Miniatures in a shadow box   58
Sepia-toned case   60
Wattle tin tray   62
Suppliers   64
Index   64

Introduction

When the idea of a book on Australian découpage was first suggested, my initial reaction was that it was an impossible task which could never be completed. Primarily I couldn't imagine that there would be enough versatility in the source of paper images that would be available and secondly I reasoned that I would never find suitably Australian objects to découpage.

A totally negative attitude ... because once I began to *see* rather than just *look at* the Australian paper products that were available I was amazed at the huge range. Then I worried that all the designs would feature either kangaroos or koalas, and again I was wrong, because some of the papers had very attractive patterns of wildflowers, country buildings, birds, cartoon characters and landscapes. These could be used singly or combined with others to achieve some very pleasing results.

As for suitable objects to découpage, I found a great source of Australiana in the Army Surplus stores, antique shops, swap meets and flea markets and the humble back shed! Many traditional items of Australiana lend themselves to being transferred by découpage—for example, an ordinary tin billy, a modern kerosene lamp, garden pots and a jarrah letterbox.

Australian découpage is exciting because of the many moods that it encompasses. It can be light and fanciful with cartoon koalas and cheeky kookaburras, rich and colourful with photographic images of wildflowers, sedate and serious with the use of sepia tones, and yet pretty, almost Victorian, with painted birds and flowers, quaint old buildings and pastel seashells.

Having realised the extent of the potential in Australian découpage, I feel that anybody who wishes to challenge the theory that it cannot be achieved will find, as I did, immense pleasure and satisfaction in the discovery that it most definitely can!

All the manufacturers of the wrapping papers, cards, books and calendars which I used are more than willing to pass on the names and addresses of local stockists of particular patterned papers to anyone wishing to inquire; for this reason I have listed the sample name or number where it is applicable. Where I have used mixed pictures from books, cards, wrapping paper, travel brochures, calendars and glossy magazines, I have not included specific information.

History of découpage

The art of découpage (derived from the French word *découper* meaning 'to cut out') involves cutting out paper motifs and images, gluing them to a hard surface and covering them several times with a clear varnish. The varnish is sanded back after many layers and the surface is then polished, creating an illusion that the paper cut-outs have been submerged in a glassy finish.

Découpage was extremely popular in eighteenth century France before finding its way across the Channel to England in the early nineteenth century. Initially découpage was an inexpensive imitation of the lacquered furniture imported from Japan, and was often referred to as 'japanning'.

During the Victorian era other paper images developed, including advertising material, scrapbook pictures and greeting cards, which lent themselves to a new form of the traditional découpage. The original time-consuming methods gave way to merely glueing paper motifs onto hard surfaces with a few coats of varnish to seal the colours. However, to achieve the original depth of image there are no shortcuts.

Modern découpage can refer to the traditional method, to decorating objects with paper cut-outs and a few coats of sealer or to merely trimming with pictures.

Materials

While the traditional craft of découpage demands a great amount of preparation using several different grades of sandpaper and many layers of varnishing and polishing, I found that some of the diverse projects in this book did not warrant such attention. The end result is still attractive and suitable for gifts, projects for the home and outdoors, stationery and other decorations without going into the time-consuming effort and some of the specialist materials required for traditional découpage.

Découpage requires a number of basic materials, but many of these can be found among inexpensive household items, with the addition of a few purchased découpage paints, brushes, sealers and other mediums.

Acrylic paints

These are obtainable from both craft and art suppliers and come in a range of colours, sizes and brands. Some of the more common brands available in Australia are Duncan acrylic paints, Folk Art acrylic colour and Jo Sonja acrylic paints. Acrylic paints are also obtainable in solid metal colours such as silver, gold, copper and brass.

Acrylic sealers

It is important when using wrapping paper, greeting cards and pictures from travel brochures in découpage that the ink in the paper be sealed. This is to prevent the colours 'bleeding' out of the pictures or, worse still, the clear gloss enamel leaking in, turning an attractive cut-out into a grey and totally unrecognisable blob. Once again there are many reliable sealers on the market, with perhaps Liquitex Gloss Medium and Varnish being the most easily obtainable.

Crackling medium

This is a clear gummy-type medium which is applied over the base coat of paint to make the second coat crack, revealing the colour beneath. The result is a weathering effect which can be quite attractive on wooden objects. Jo Sonja has a very good crackling medium, as do Duncan with their Quik Crackle. Both of these are readily available from craft stores.

Glue

Each project requires a specific type of glue; for instance, cut-out pictures on stationery need a paper glue. I recommend a good quality glue stick which adheres without running everywhere and marking the background card. With very finely cut out pictures, however, a glue stick will rip the paper, so a glue pencil with a small roller in the head is recommended. I find the craft glue in a small bottle the best type to stick motifs onto tins and porous pots, while a mixture of three parts Clag glue with one part PVA woodworking glue makes a slow drying but reliable glueing agent for wooden and papier-mâché items.

Clear gloss enamels

The clear gloss enamels which are used to varnish the finished découpage are available from hardware stores, paint suppliers and major department stores. The products which have proven themselves to be most reliable include Estapol High Gloss, MonoCel

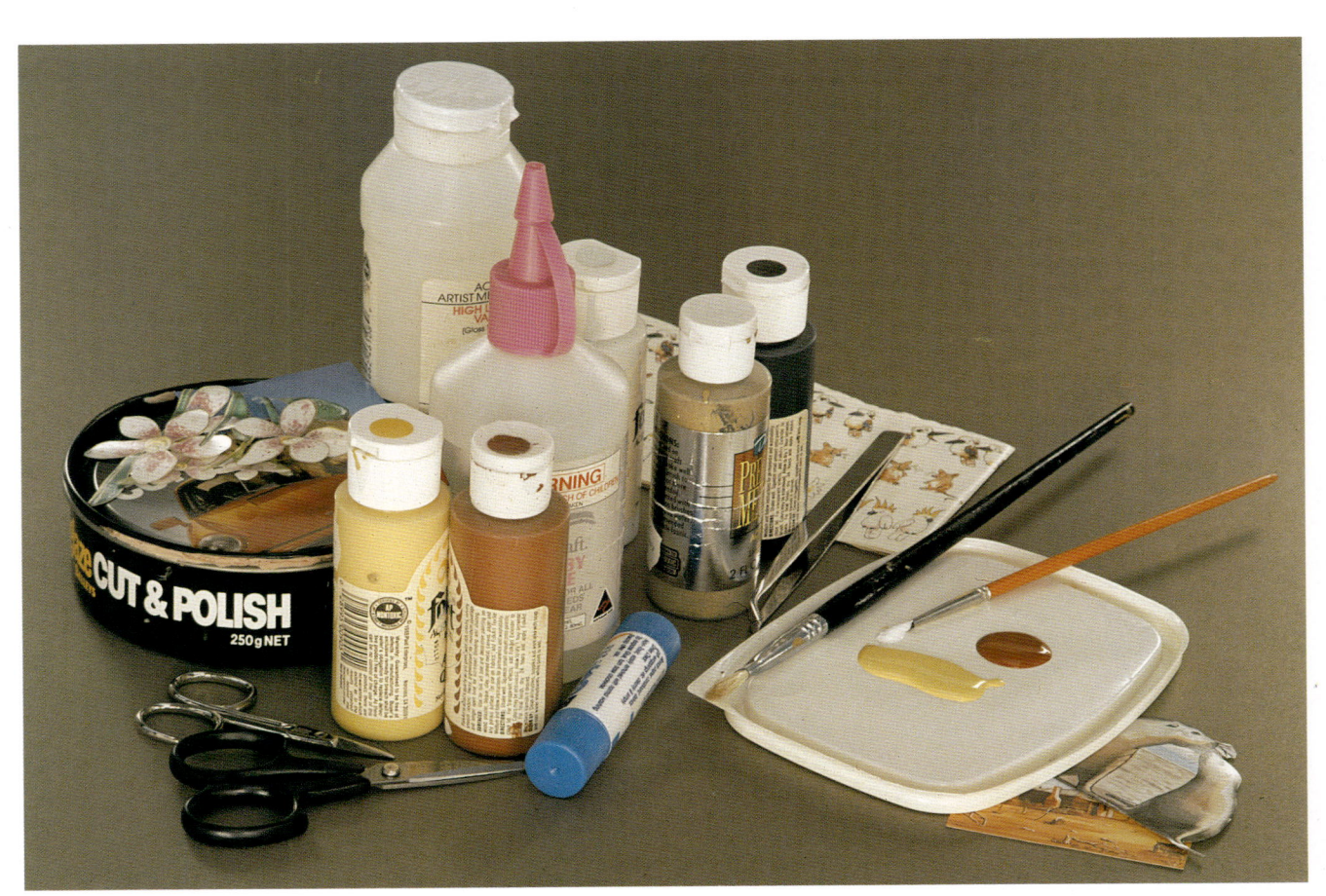

Materials used in découpage

Polyurethane Ultra Gloss and Walpamur Indoor/Outoor Varnish.

Brushes

The size of the brushes required obviously depends upon the object being painted, sealed or varnished at the time, but the quality is most important. Cost is not always the most reliable way of judging quality, as I have paid a lot of money for a brush that felt good but which lost hairs all over my work, while another small brush which cost me 50 cents from a craft store was really great. Generally, brushes bought from a craft or art supplier are better than a general-purpose small brush from a hardware shop.

Turpentine

A most important item to have on hand, as brushes must be cleaned immediately after use so that they remain soft, clean and pliable. The best way to store brushes between use is in the turpentine itself, flicking away the excess before using them again. Once the turpentine becomes discoloured or gluggy, throw it away and replace it with clean liquid. Don't keep it too long with the brushes standing in it or the residue from several washes of paint will settle in the bottom of the jar and clog the brushes. If possible, suspend the brushes from a hole in the lid or hang them from a hook above the jar by a length of cord. This is especially suitable if the brush has a hanging loop at the end.

Scissors

Several types of scissors are required for various aspects of découpage, but they must be *sharp*. The cutting-out of the small and sometimes intricate paper images is the most important part of the process and can make the difference between an excellent piece of découpage and a piece which is decidedly substandard. A pair of long pointed scissors is necessary for cutting into the paper to separate a particular motif from the background or for removing larger areas of the plain paper before using a small pair of scissors with very sharp curved blades to remove all the tiny pieces of background paper. Craft scissors are useful for cutting thicker card, ribbons, lining fabrics and other trimmings.

Household items

There are many household items which are used or can be utilised.

Steel wool   Used to rub down any rough spots on tins.

Kitchen sponge   The one which I prefer to use when applying stipple paint or the final layer of paint in crackling is a plain square of fine yellow sponge.

Palette   Some of the most useful items to keep for adapting into palettes are the lids of icecream containers. Once the acrylic paint is finished with it can be washed off, even if it has been allowed to harden, and the palette used again and again.

Another very useful idea for a palette is a board covered with clear plastic kitchen wrap. Once the painting process has been completed you can roll up the plastic wrap with the dried paint inside and discard it.

Empty acrylic paint bottles   These make very suitable small rollers for pressing out air bubbles from beneath glued paper cut-outs. Remove the top of the bottle and wash out all left-over paint before leaving to dry thoroughly both inside and out.

Blu-tack   Comes in very handy when the paper motifs are being arranged to fit into a certain shape. The Blu-tack can be easily rubbed off the back of the motifs before they are glued to the object permanently.

Soft cloths for wiping   I have found that the best lint-free cloths for wiping away excess glue or for pressing out air bubbles are old cotton or linen tea-towels which have lost all their excess lint and fluff, and old (and very washed out) tee shirts. When tee shirts have lost all the lint particles with repeated washing they make extremely soft wipers.

Sandpaper   Especially the wet-and-dry type. Used for coarse-sanding wooden items before they are painted and for fine-sanding finished articles after they have had at least twenty coats of varnish and before they are polished. I recommend the 400, 600 and 1200 grades.

Sources of Australian paper motifs

Wrapping paper

There is an amazing choice of Australian designs in wrapping paper, which is available in both newsagents and card shops as well as by mail order. The manufacturers of the wrapping papers used in this book will be happy to supply you with details of the nearest stockist of their individual papers.

Sources of Australian découpage material

Greetings cards
Manufacturers are becoming more aware of the growing demand for cards with motifs depicting Australian animals, wildflowers and landscapes, particularly at Christmas time. Packs of suitable cards are available in variety stores with an assortment of drawings, photographs and paintings.

Books
While it is hard to cut out the pages of good books, many books available from library clearance sales, secondhand shops and warehouse clearances are cheap and quite suitable for découpage. If a book is bought specifically as a supply of cut-out pictures then your conscience should be clear about cutting into it!

Calendars
Once the beginning of a new year has passed many shops sell their pictorial, photographic and hand-drawn calendars for half price. This is the time to buy them for cutting up, particularly as some projects need repeated images and calendars can often be purchased in twos and threes at these times. Of course, last year's used calendar is more than adequate as well, as long as you have not written on the backs of the pictures.

Découpage paper
Now that découpage is established as a recognised craft, many designers are creating papers especially for cutting up. While a lot of these designs are Victorian motifs, flowers and teddybears, many more manufacturers are catering for the purely Australian image. These companies advertise in craft magazines and most have mail order facilities.

Travel brochures
These are available free from all travel agencies and provide a source of bright and colourful photographic pictures of every state in the country. Some also have pencil sketches of a particular town or tourist attraction which can be coordinated into a découpage design with coloured pictures.

Other images
Certain types of paper products such as postage stamps, photographs, magazine advertisements and labels from tins of fruit, packets of jelly and even jars of Vegemite will be very useful in the art of découpage, filling in background areas and blending with other pictures to create an all-over design with an Australian flavour.

Terracotta pots

These terracotta pots were not new from the nursery or garden centre—they were rescued from the backyard after months, even years, of neglect. Obviously they were covered in dirt and grime which had to be removed before anything else could be attempted; in the case of one particular pot which had been half submerged in the soil, damp mouldy areas had to be thoroughly dried out.

Terracotta pots are undoubtedly the most attractive containers for pot plants and lend themselves most successfully to recycling, as these examples prove.

Materials
One or more terracotta pots
Sponge and scourer
Mild detergent or soap powder

Terracotta pots

Acrylic paint
Liquitex acrylic varnish
Craft glue
Suitable pictures or wrapping paper
Sharp-pointed small scissors
Estapol or MonoCel Clear Gloss paint
Small soft-bristled brush and larger brush for the clear gloss
Turpentine

Large pot

Sample paper Eucalypts by Pettis Studios.

Choose a warm sunny day to clean the pot, as it needs to be dried quickly to avoid any further dampness.

Directions
1. Soak the pot in hot water and detergent, then scrub clean using the scourer and sponge, making sure that there is no soil or plant residue clinging to the inside. Rinse away all trace of the detergent.
2. Dry as thoroughly as possible with a clean cloth. An old linen tea-towel is ideal for this as all of the excess lint and fluff has long gone. Do not use a cloth made from towelling which will leave lint and cotton caught in the rough surface. Leave out in direct sunlight to dry out completely.
3. Using acrylic paint in a rust or terracotta colour, cover the pot both inside and out with two coats, leaving the surface to dry thoroughly between coats.
4. Carefully cut out the chosen paper images from cards or wrapping paper and smear the backs and fronts of each with a sealer such as the Liquitex varnish. Let the sealer dry.
5. When enough pictures have been sealed arrange them around the bottom portion of the pot only and glue them in place with craft glue or with a mixture of PVA and Clag glues (Fig. 1).
6. Cut out and seal smaller paper images to be glued around the lip of the pot, placing motifs around the lower edge of the lip to overhang the cut edges of the first pictures (Fig. 2).
7. When all the glue is dry, cover the pot with the clear gloss, making absolutely sure that all the overhanging cut-outs are coated underneath as well. Give the pot two or three coats of the gloss, allowing at least twelve hours for each coat to dry.
8. It is extremely important to cover the pot both inside and out with the gloss enamel to waterproof the paper images. Make sure that even the drainage hole at the bottom has been coated with the two

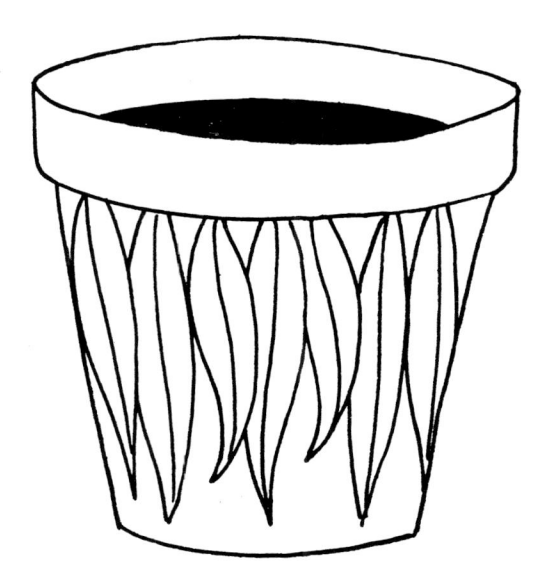

Fig. 1. Apply a generous coating of glue to the backs of the paper motifs to be stuck to the body of the pot. Remove any air bubbles by pressing with a soft cloth. Cut the motifs straight across the top so they will fit flush against the pot just underneath the lip.

Fig. 2. Once the glue on the motifs which have been stuck to the pot has dried, apply a coat of sealer and clear gloss enamel. Glue motifs around the bottom of the lip of the pot, leaving them overhanging the edge. In this manner the new motifs will hide the top edges of the previous ones.

or three coats of enamel varnish, otherwise the moisture will seep through the pottery to the underside of the pictures, making them white and soggy.

Medium pot

Sample paper Evelyn Studios No. BW04.

Directions
1. Prepare the pot in the same way as the large one to the painting stage. Paint the bottom portion and the inside of the pot in rust or terracotta coloured paint. Paint the upper lip in a dark green, once again applying two coats with at least two hours drying time between coats of paint.
2. With the small sharp pointed scissors, cut small paper images from wrapping paper and seal them on both sides with a coat of acrylic sealer. Check that the pictures are small enough to sit smoothly around the top lip of the pot.
3. When the sealer on the pictures has dried, carefully glue them evenly spaced around the green band. Cover this upper lip with another coat of sealer.
4. Once this coat is dry, apply two or three coats of gloss enamel, allowing at least twelve hours between each one. Make sure that the entire pot, including the drainage hole at the bottom, has been covered with the layers of gloss enamel to waterproof the pictures from moisture seeping through from the inside.

Small pot

Sample paper Pettis Studios Australian Daisies.

Directions
1. Prepare the pot in the same manner as the two larger ones and paint the surface both inside and out with two layers of rust or terracotta coloured acrylic paint, allowing at least two hours drying time between coats.
2. Carefully cut out enough paper images from wrapping paper or a book to completely cover the entire pot. Cut away any white or coloured background paper which shows between the motifs, such as between the petals of the sample paper.
3. Paint a coat of acrylic sealer on both sides of each paper motif and allow it time to dry thoroughly. Beginning at the bottom of the pot, glue pictures all the way around, overlapping the edges. Work up the sides of the pot, gradually covering the surface until the upper lip is reached.
4. Glue a row of pictures around this upper portion and when the glue has dried completely, attach another line of motifs, overlapping the previous ones. Snip into the bottom edges of these motifs and press them securely over the ridge of the lip.
5. When the glue is thoroughly dry, apply a coat of clear gloss to completely cover the pot both inside and out. Leave to dry for at least twelve hours before applying a second and third coat.

Three tins with different finishes

Painted metal surfaces
The three tins which I have used as samples have each been covered by a different method. Each tin is attractive and individual and has been decorated accordingly.

Plain painted tin The first tin with the animals design was simply coated with three coats of acrylic paint before the pictures were glued to the sides and lid. In some cases this plain surface is sufficient.

Stippled tin The black and gold tin with the shell pattern on the lid and around the bottom has been stippled. Stippling means painting the tin first with a layer or two of undercoat then sponging on a highlight colour—in this case, gold. The sponge needs to be fine in texture and very dry to touch. Smear the gold paint lightly on the surface of the sponge and dab evenly over the entire surface of the tin. Do not press too firmly or coat the sponge too thickly with paint or the end result will be gold blobs rather than a speckled look.

Crackled tin The gold tin has been crackled with a crackling medium. I used Duncan's Quik Crackle but there are several equally good brands on the market. Cover the tin and the lid with two coats of base coat, leaving two hours drying time between coats. Cover the areas to be crackled (I left the band around the edge of the lid free) with an even coating of the crackling medium and leave for forty minutes to one hour to set. With a piece of fine sponge which has been dabbed into a second colour of acrylic paint, quickly and firmly press it completely over the crackled surface. Do not be tempted to cover the spots which will appear almost immediately with the second colour of paint, as it is more than likely that the crackling process has already begun. Leave for at least three hours for the crackling to cease then seal with an acrylic sealer. The tin is now ready for the pictures to be glued on.

Baby animals tin

Sample paper Baby Animals paper by Card Sharp.

Materials
Small tin with lid
Acrylic paint
Suitable paper to cut out motifs
Liquitex varnish
Estapol or MonoCel Clear Gloss Enamel
Soft-bristled artist's brush and
 larger brush for clear gloss
Turpentine
Craft glue or a mixture of PVA and Clag

Directions
1. Check that the tin has no rust spots or burrs. If there are any rough areas, rub gently with a small piece of steel wool and apply a small coating of anti-rust paint.
2. Once the surface is free of rough spots, paint with a coat of acrylic paint. Wait at least two hours before applying another coat and even a third coat. This will be necessary if the tin had a previous pattern of dark or very bright colours.
3. Carefully cut out enough paper motifs to be spaced evenly around the tin itself and to be arranged into a suitable design on the lid (Fig. 3).
4. It may help at this stage to stick the pictures in place temporarily with tiny pieces of Blu-tack until they are uniformly spaced around the tin. Having removed the Blu-tack, paint each picture on both

Baby animals tin

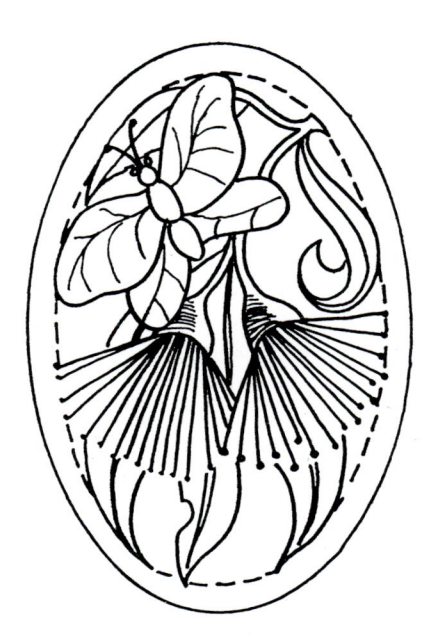

Fig. 3. To arrange pictures on the lid of a tin, imagine a line going around the edge about 5 to 10 mm (¼'' – ½'') from the outside. Use this imaginary line as the outer limit of the paper cut-outs which will create a uniform design.

Fig. 4. When glueing motifs around a tin which has a separate lid, mark lightly where the bottom edge of the lid will reach down the side. Do not apply any paper motifs above this line.

Stippled black and gold shell tin

sides with an acrylic sealer, let dry and glue them down onto the tin, pressing out any small air bubbles which may appear (Fig. 4).
5. Seal the picture areas with another coat of acrylic sealer. Once this is dry, apply one coat of the clear gloss enamel and allow at least twelve hours drying time. Apply another ten coats of gloss enamel to the lid and also to the tin itself, but do not paint the area around the top of the tin which is covered by the lid. Too many coats of varnish around this top edge and the lid will not be able to slip on.

Stippled black and gold tin

Materials
Tin with lid
Black acrylic paint
Gold acrylic paint
Small piece of fine sponge
Liquitex acrylic varnish
Craft glue or a mix of PVA and Clag
Fine sharp-pointed scissors
Suitable pictures from books or paper
Clear gloss enamel
Soft-bristled artists' brushes

Directions
1. Rub the tin with fine sandpaper if there are any rust spots or small burrs and treat with a smear of rust killer if necessary.
2. Paint the tin and the lid with three coats of black base coat, allowing at least two or three hours drying time between each application.
3. When the base coat is completely dry, squeeze a little of the gold paint onto a palette and smear a light coating onto the surface of the dry sponge.
4. Quickly and evenly dab the sponge over the tin and the lid, smearing more paint onto the sponge as it is needed. Keep the dabbing light or your fingertips will create gold blobs instead of the speckled look that is required.
5. Wait two hours until the gold coat has dried before painting the entire surface with an acrylic sealer such as Liquitex.

6. Carefully cut out the chosen paper motifs to cover the lid and to be arranged in a border around the sides. Coat each motif with acrylic sealer; when they have completely dried place them in position with a tiny piece of Blu-tack. In this way the images can be moved around until the design is satisfactory.
7. Using either craft glue or a mixture of PVA and Clag, glue the motifs onto the lid and around the bottom edge. Coat again with a layer of acrylic sealer.
8. Apply six to ten layers of clear gloss enamel to the lid but only one coat on the tin itself. Mark off where the lid is going to slide over the tin and apply another five to ten coats of gloss below this line. If the top edge of the tin is coated too thickly with the gloss, the lid will not slip on easily or, once forced on, will not budge again and the end result will be a very attractive, but permanently closed tin!

Crackled heart butterfly tin

Sample papers Pettis Studios Pink Flowering Gum paper; butterflies from Sheet No. 1761 of Mamelok Press scrapbook pictures.

Materials
Small tin with a lid
Pictures for the lid and sides
Acrylic base paint
Soft-bristled artist's brush
Stiffer bristled brush for crackling
Gold acrylic paint
Liquitex acrylic varnish
Clear gloss enamel
10 mm wide satin ribbon to fit around the lid
10 mm wide satin ribbon to make a bow
Craft glue
Small piece of fine sponge and sharp-pointed scissors

Directions
1. Smooth any rusty spots or rough patches on the surface of the tin with fine sandpaper and treat any rust with an anti-rust paint.
2. Allowing two hours drying time between coats, apply two or three coats of rust or terracotta coloured acrylic base paint to the tin and the lid.
3. When this is thoroughly dry, cover the lid and the sides of the tin with an even coat of Quik Crackle. Leave this to set for forty minutes to one hour.
4. Squeeze some of the gold acrylic paint onto a palette and dab the sponge into it or, for a lighter coating of gold, brush the paint onto the sponge with a brush. Quickly and smoothly dab the sponge over the entire crackled surface of the lid and the tin. Signs of crackling should show almost immediately.
5. Leave for at least three to four hours to dry thoroughly. Crackling will continue for about one and a half hours. Carefully cut out suitable paper motifs to cover the top and to arrange around the sides of the tin. Paint both sides of each motif with a sealer and leave to dry.
6. Space the smaller motifs evenly around the sides using tiny pieces of Blu-tack, moving them about until the design is satisfactory. Glue them in place with either craft glue or a mixture of PVA and Clag.
7. When the glue has dried completely, seal once again with a coat of sealer. Apply at least six coats of clear gloss enamel, leaving twelve hours drying time between coats.
8. Measure accurately around the lip of the lid and cut the ribbon 3 mm longer to overlap. Squeeze a small amount of craft glue around the edge of the lid and, starting from the back, press the ribbon in position.
9. Tie a small bow from the ribbon and glue to the front of the lid.

Butterfly tin

Postage stamp desk set

Postage stamps have a way of accumulating once they have been used, filling tins and boxes and remaining hidden in drawers. This set was my husband Eddie's idea of how to display his own collection of used postage stamps and enjoy the effort of arranging them at the same time. Having never showed much aptitude for craft before, he is particularly pleased with the result. The stamps are available in large bags of mixed varieties which need to be soaked in warm water to remove the torn portion of envelope which is invariably glued to the back. It is best to soak a small number of stamps at any one time so that they do not stay in the water for too long and become soggy. The containers onto which the dry stamps were then glued were an unrelated group consisting of a wooden box with a spray of painted flowers on the lid, a papier-mâché round caddy which originally had a fitted top and a small hard-covered address book from a variety store.

Materials
Suitable hard containers such as wooden or papier-mâché boxes, small tins with or without lids, hard-covered notebooks or address books
Glue—mixture of Clag and white PVA woodworking glue
Liquitex acrylic varnish
Craft knife or Stanley trimmer
Acrylic paint for undercoat, preferably black
Fine sandpaper
A large quantity of used postage stamps
Clear gloss enamel such as MonoCel or Estapol

Directions
1. Carefully sandpaper the surface of any boxes or containers which have rough surfaces or small burrs until they are smooth. Wipe off dust.

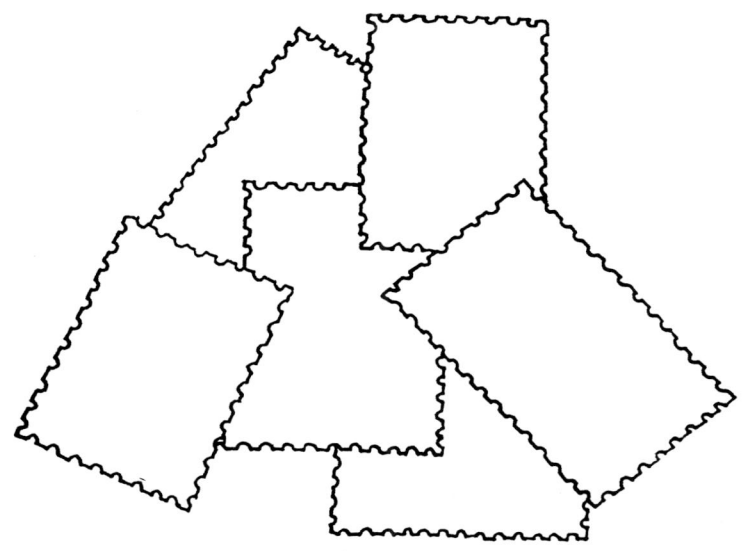

Fig. 5. Glue the stamps onto the box by overlapping the edges of each one, making sure that there are no spaces left between them where the base wood shows through.

2. Paint all containers with the undercoat both inside and out. Paint the cover of the notebook carefully, making sure that the paint does not touch the inside pages.
3. Put the lid on the box and glue stamps over the top and all four sides, overlapping them. Wipe out any excess glue or air bubbles as you go until there are no spaces showing. The lid at this stage is glued onto the box by the covering of stamps (Fig. 5).
4. Leave overnight or even longer to dry. Do not touch the box again until you are sure that all the stamps are completely dried out.
5. Carefully slice around the lid with the craft knife or Stanley trimmer to separate the lid from the box. This method provides the two pieces with a

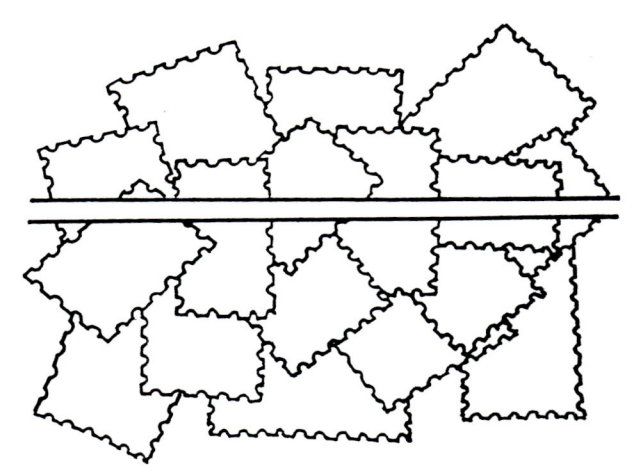

Fig. 6. Glue the stamps onto the box while the lid is still in place. When it has dried completely, slice the gap between the box and the lid with a craft knife. This will ensure that the stamps make a perfect match when the lid is on the box.

perfectly matching design when the lid is placed back in position (Fig. 6).

6. Cover the box and lid surfaces with a coat of acrylic varnish and press the cut edges flat with the fingers. Where any white edges show, colour with a black pencil or felt pen which will not leak ink when varnished.
7. Cover with three coats of acrylic varnish, leaving at least two hours drying time in between coats.
8. Finally, apply at least twenty coats of clear gloss enamel to all pieces, allowing at least twelve hours between coats so that they dry thoroughly.
9. Either finely sandpaper the surface then polish with a beeswax polish until the correct shine is achieved, or polish with a car cutting and polishing compound and finish with a coat of silicone glaze.

Australian stamps desk set

Gum blossom wooden dressing table set

Sample papers Pink Flowering Gum paper from Pettis Studios; the kingfishers come from the book *What Bird is That?* by Neville Cayley.

The wooden items used in this project were all treated in the same manner which meant that each step on the different pieces could be done at the same time. The wooden pieces were obtained by mail order in Australia from Timber Turn, whose address appears in the suppliers list at the back of this book.

There are unlimited ideas for decorating a set of matching articles such as these, using pastel, black or plain dark-coloured backgrounds. The cut-outs could be Victorian images of cupids, roses and hearts, brightly coloured animal motifs suitable for children or with a completely natural theme like those in the sample.

The beauty of creating your own decorator pieces is the versatility of the colour schemes and the vast range of suitable paper cut-out ideas. This set also makes a lovely gift, either singly or together, and would be greatly appreciated.

Materials
Wooden tissue box
Wooden photo frame
Small wooden box, round, oval or heart-shaped
Acrylic paint for the background
Suitable pictures from paper, books or cards
Small finely-pointed scissors
Craft glue
Gold acrylic paint
Acrylic sealer such as Liquitex
Clear gloss enamel such as Estapol or MonoCel
Fine gold braid to fit around the inside of the oval on the photograph frame. The braid in the sample was bought from a newsagents for use in tying presents. It came on a slim reel
Velvet ribbon to fit around the lid of the box
Small piece of kitchen sponge
Small piece of fine sandpaper, wet-and-dry 600

Photograph frame

Directions
1. Check first whether the photograph frame is one in which the photo slides down a gap at the top, one in which the oval in the centre is pushed out or one which is a solid shape for which the photograph needs to be cut to size. If it is the second type, remove the oval.
2. Sand the frame to remove any rough edges, small burrs or loose splinters of wood. Wipe down with a soft cloth to remove any sanding dust.
3. Paint the frame with two or three coats of the acrylic paint, leaving at least two hours drying time between coats. Paint the back of the frame too, and the small piece of wood usually provided as a stand support.
4. Using the small scissors, carefully cut away all the background paper moù between the motifs. In this case, although it is time-consuming and fiddly, the end result will be well worth the patient effort. Using small pieces of Blu-tack, position the paper motifs around the oval. It may help to draw around the frame onto a piece of paper which can be used as a template. The pictures can then be arranged on the paper.
5. Using the craft glue or a mixture of Clag and PVA glue carefully secure the motifs in position, wiping away any excess glue and pressing out air bubbles as you progress with a soft cloth.

Gum blossom wooden dressing table set

23

6. Leave these pictures for at least three or four hours to dry thoroughly, as when paper images are overlapped, drying takes longer than usual. Using the gold paint and a small stiff brush, carefully paint around the edges of the frame, wiping away any stray brushes of gold immediately. With care and patience it is possible to achieve a perfectly straight edge.

7. Cover the entire frame with a coating of the acrylic sealer. Once this has dried, after approximately two hours, apply twenty coats of varnish, leaving the frame overnight between coats.

8. The frame can be left highly varnished or lightly sandpapered down to remove all traces of the shine. Once this is completed, apply a beeswax polish. Another alternative is to rub down the surface with a car polish which has a cutting ingredient such as Selleys Cut and Polish, then polish with a silicone glaze.

9. The frame itself is now finished. Assemble the photo according to the instructions (the sample photograph had to be cut to the oval template) and using the craft glue, adhere the fine gold braid or cord around the edge with the join at the bottom.

Tissue box

Directions

1. Sandpaper all the rough edges from the tissue box in the same manner as for the photograph frame and wipe off any excess dust with a soft cloth.
2. Apply two or three coats of the acrylic paint leaving at least two hours drying time between coats.
3. Carefully cut out all the paper motifs making sure that every piece of background has been removed.
4. Arrange the paper cut-outs on the box top. Once the design has been satisfactorily positioned, begin glueing them in place. Work out from the oval in the centre of the tissue box and gradually take the cut-out pieces over the side edge.
5. Arrange and glue the main motifs onto the two long sides which will become the front and the back, then the two ends, overlapping pieces where necessary.
6. Once all the glueing has been completed and allowed to dry out completely, paint the box with a coating of the acrylic sealer. Allow another two hours for this to dry.
7. Using the gold acrylic paint, carefully paint the lip around the inner edge of the oval centre. Once again cover with the sealer when it is dry.

8. Cover the entire box with twenty coats of clear gloss enamel, leaving at least twelve hours drying time between coats, preferably overnight.
9. After the paper images have been 'sunk' beneath all these layers of varnish, either sandpaper the surface lightly or rub over with Selleys Cut and Polish. Polish the sanded surface with beeswax polish or use a silicone glaze.

Trinket box

Directions

1. Prepare the box lid and body by sanding smooth with the sandpaper. Wipe clean with a soft cloth to remove any excess dust.
2. Paint both pieces inside and out with three coats of the acrylic paint, leaving at least two hours drying time between coats. The inside bottom of the box may even take longer to be completely dry.
3. Cut out the paper motifs and arrange onto the top of the lid only, overlapping the pieces so that they create a circular design.
4. With the small piece of sponge stipple the base and sides of the box by squeezing a little of the gold acrylic paint onto a palette and dabbing the sponge into this. Wipe off any excess paint so that the sponge is almost dry.
5. Quickly, evenly and most importantly lightly, dab the sponge over the box bottom and around the sides. Stand the box upside-down for two or three hours until it is completely dry.
6. Cover both the box and the lid with a layer of the acrylic sealer and leave again for two hours.
7. Using the clear gloss enamel, apply one coat over the box and lid. When this coat is dry after being left overnight, mark where the lid comes down over the sides of the box. Do not apply any more varnish over this mark, or the lid will not slide on and off easily.
8. Leaving for at least twelve hours between coats of gloss enamel, apply another nineteen coats until the paper images have been sunk underneath.
9. Carefully sandpaper the sides and base of the box, being very gentle because heavy pressure on this type of wood can make it crack. Alternatively, rub Selleys Cut and Polish over the box with a soft cloth until there is no shine left. Polish with either beeswax polish or a silicone glaze.
10. Finally, apply the craft glue around the lip of the box lid and press the ribbon firmly in position, starting and finishing at the back. Cut off any excess ribbon as you do not want the two ends to overlap.

Barrier Reef brick doorstop

Sample paper Barrier Reef Fish by Card Sharp.

What better use to put a humble housebrick left over from a building project to than to découpage it with paper to match the theme of a room and prop it against a slamming door? The type of brick best suited for this purpose is the plain solid sort, one that has no holes or indentations. The average size of a brick is 23.5 cm × 11 cm × 8 cm (9¼″ × 4½″ × 3⅛″); two sheets of any type of découpage or wrapping paper are needed to obtain enough paper cut-outs to cover all sides.

Barrier Reef brick doorstop

Materials
One housebrick without holes
2 sheets suitable wrapping paper or découpage paper
Acrylic undercoat paint
Clear gloss enamel
Acrylic sealer and varnish
Mixture of 3 parts Clag and 1 part PVA glue
Square of felt for the base
Small sharp-pointed scissors

Directions
1. Scrape any lumps and bumps from the sides of the brick and remove any dirt or paint flakes.
2. Once the brick is clean and smooth, paint with two coats of acrylic paint, leaving for at least three hours to dry.
3. Begin glueing the pictures to the brick by placing a large piece of background paper on the top. In this case I used a piece of plain watery blue paper. Starting from the bottom edge on all four sides lay the pictures overlapping one another and with approximately 1 cm (½") motif over the edge. Glue these into place, folding the spare paper over the bottom edge and pressing down firmly. This bottom side will be covered by the felt.
4. Glue the pictures around the top edge of the brick, once again bringing the motifs over the sides of the brick on all four sides. Fill in the centre of each side with overlapping motifs, and apply some others to the top over the background paper (Fig. 7).
5. Cover the top, ends and sides of the brick with the acrylic sealer to protect the colours in the paper from being soaked in the varnish.
6. Once the sealer has dried completely, apply ten coats of the gloss enamel, leaving overnight to dry between coats.
7. If you desire a more mellow sheen, rub the brick with a soft cloth dipped in Selleys Polyglaze Cut and Polish to remove all the shine. Polish with a silicone polish.
8. Smear glue over the whole bottom surface of the doorstop brick, then place it firmly into the square of felt. Place a heavy weight on top so that the felt adheres evenly and securely.
9. Once this glue is dry (leave for twenty-four hours), carefully cut away any felt from around the edges, leaving only the bottom surface covered.

Fig. 7. Glue a large piece of background paper to the top of the brick, then cover the edges with motifs. Glue motifs around the bottom edge of the brick, then fill in the spaces around the four sides.

Billy kitchen tool container

The common old billy has long been associated with Australia's folklore, ever since the swagman watched and waited for his to boil in 'Waltzing Matilda'; all Australians have heard of billy tea and damper, the billy being an integral part of droving life.

It wasn't necessary to scour old campsites looking for a left-over billy to create this sample as the Army Surplus stores have brand new ones in plentiful supply. The pictures were a bit more of a challenge to collect, but there are many suitable sources when you start to look around, including advertisements from old magazines and even jam and tinned fruit labels.

Sample paper Wildflowers and birds in stained glass from Aqua Unicorn Images Pty Ltd, and an assortment of other paper motifs. The wildflower and birds paper is an excellent paper to use to fill in the gaps between other motifs as the bright colours blend in beautifully, creating a uniform cover.

Materials
One billycan with handle
Acrylic paint
Sharp-pointed small scissors
Clear gloss enamel
Liquitex sealer and varnish

Directions
1. Paint the billycan inside and out with the acrylic paint. Because of the new silver metal surface it may be necessary to apply up to four coats of paint to the billy, hinges and handle before it is completely covered. Leave up to two hours between coats.
2. Carefully cut out a large assortment of pictures covering all aspects of Australia, making sure that there is no white background paper left even in small areas. Cut out many more motifs than you will eventually require.
3. Because the pictures have come from a variety of different sources and may not be leak-proof, it is necessary to paint each and every motif with the acrylic sealer on both the back and front. While this is time-consuming it is imperative, otherwise varnish could leak into the pictures, making them totally unrecognisable, or ink could leak out, creating a faded colourless image.
4. Once the pictures have completely dried, they can be glued onto the billy, overlapping the edges of each one so that the colours merge. Begin glueing from underneath the lip at the top of the can, cutting around the handle hinges.
5. Now glue a row of pictures around the bottom edge, overlapping them in a similar manner to the top row. Keeping the largest and most attractive cut-outs until last, fill the middle area, once again overlapping the pictures over the top and bottom rows until the surface has been covered.
6. Cover the surface with another layer of the acrylic sealer and leave for three or four hours to dry. It will take longer than usual because of all the layers of paper.
7. Apply up to twenty coats of a gloss enamel (such as Estapol or MonoCel), leaving at least twelve hours, preferably overnight, between coats. The inside of the tin and the hinges and handle will only require four or five coats.
8. Rub over the can with Selleys Cut and Polish on a soft cloth or lightly sandpaper the surface until there is no shine left. Polish with either a beeswax polish or a silicone glaze.

Illustrated on page 28

Billy kitchen tool container

Lampshade base and photo frame

Sample paper Small Animals and Wildflowers from Card Sharp.

This project was undertaken primarily to recycle a rather ugly circa 1970s teak lampshade base. The photograph frame was a commercial 26 cm × 20.5 cm (10″ × 8″) frame which included the cardboard mount, but any size frame would be suitable for this type of undertaking provided that the cardboard mount is large enough to take the paper cut-outs glued onto the surface.

Materials
Lampshade base
Commercial photograph frame with a cardboard mount. If a cardboard mount is not available, cut a piece of cardboard to match the size of the backing board, measure 4 cm (1½″) in from the outside edges and cut out a central rectangular aperture with a craft knife
Small piece of clean kitchen sponge
Craft glue
Acrylic paint for the undercoat
Acrylic paint for the stippling colour
Acrylic seal such as Liquitex gloss medium and varnish
Sandpaper
Clear gloss enamel
Small sharp-pointed scissors
Soft-bristled artist's brush

Directions
1. Sandpaper the lampshade base to remove any rough spots and old varnish. Wipe away the excess dust with a clean soft cloth.
2. Apply three coats of the acrylic base-coloured paint to both the lampshade base and the cardboard mount, leaving two hours between coats.
3. Spread some of the second coloured paint onto a palette and wipe a small amount of this onto the sponge. Dab the sponge onto a piece of scrap paper to remove the excess paint, then quickly and firmly stipple the second colour lightly over the base coat.
4. Once again leave for two hours so that the paint will dry thoroughly, meanwhile cutting out the paper cut-outs from wrapping paper, removing all the background areas. Cover these cut-outs with acrylic sealer on both sides and leave to dry.
5. Glue these motifs onto the lampshade base and the photograph mount (Fig. 8). Where the lamp-

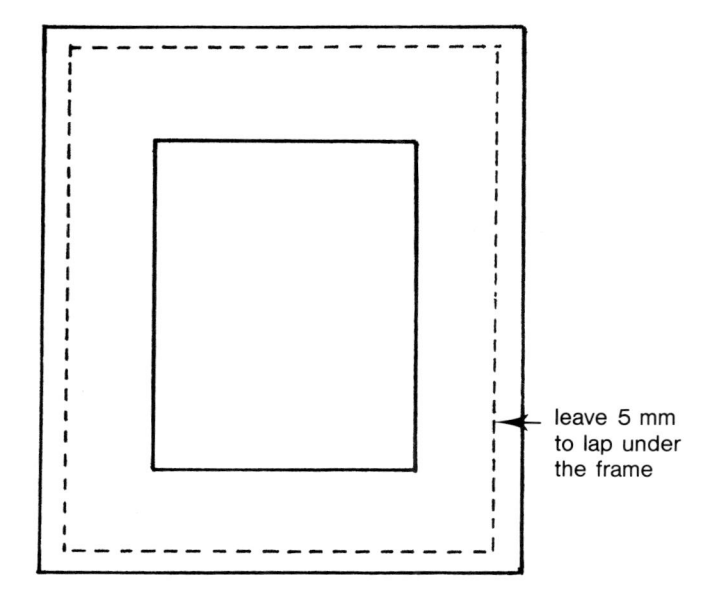

leave 5 mm to lap under the frame

Fig. 8. Cut the photograph frame mount to fit inside the commercial frame. Cut out the aperture in the centre and paint the frame. When glueing the paper cut-outs around the edge leave the outer 5 mm blank, as this will fit behind the wooden frame.

Lampshade base and photo frame

shade base is curved, snip around the edges of each motif so that it will overlap and follow the curve smoothly.

6. Cover with a coat of the acrylic gloss sealer and allow two to three hours to dry properly before adding a second coat.

7. Finally, cover with three coats of the clear gloss enamel. Leave these two items with the highly glossed surface.

Australian parrots placemats, coasters and napkin rings

Sample paper Evelyn Studios Parrot paper, No. BW23.

These placemats and coasters have been recycled from mismatched sets. The placemats had faded and scratched floral designs on the front while the coasters originally had photographic views of Perth. The serviette rings were wooden ones of similar shape, although some were pine and some were hardwood. With a coating of crackled paint and the brightly coloured parrot and wattle designs, they make a stunning table setting with an obvious Australian flavour.

Materials
Assorted cork-backed placemats, coasters and wooden serviette rings
Gold acrylic paint
Crackling medium such as Duncan's Quik Crackle
Blue or other dark-coloured acrylic paint
Paper or cards with brightly coloured paper images
Soft artist's brush
Clear gloss enamel such as Estapol or MonoCel
Liquitex acrylic varnish
Fine sharp-pointed scissors
Tweezers to hold the fine pieces of paper
600 wet-and-dry sandpaper

Directions
1. Using the sandpaper gently rub any rough patches off the surface of the mats and coasters. If they are new and glossy, use the sandpaper to break up the surface so that the paint will adhere.
2. Cover the surfaces to be crackled with a base coat of acrylic paint in blue or another dark colour. Leave for at least two hours to dry.
3. Paint on two coats of gold acrylic paint, once again leaving two or three hours of drying time between them.
4. Cover each placemat, coaster and serviette ring with an even coating of the crackling medium and leave for about 45 minutes to set.
5. Squeeze the blue paint onto a palette and dab the sponge into it, covering the surface evenly. Quickly dab the sponge over the entire surface of the gold-painted mats and coasters, putting more paint on the sponge as it becomes necessary. Crackling will begin almost immediately so do not be tempted to go over areas that have already been dabbed under the misapprehension that spots have

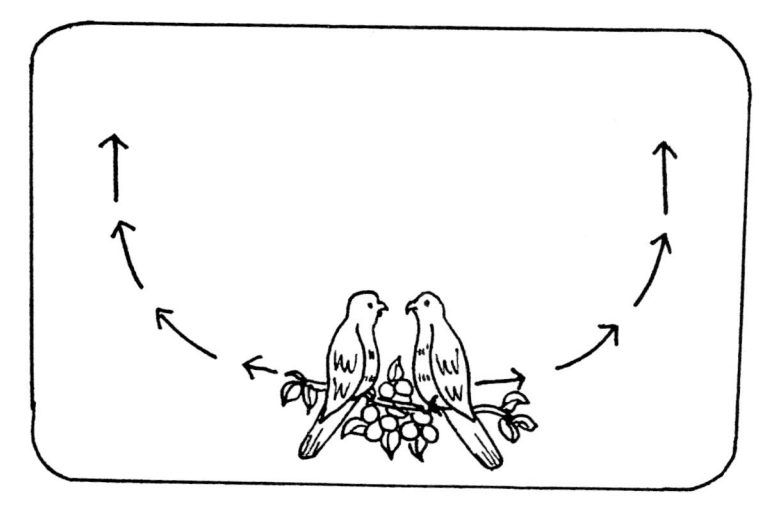

Fig. 9. Diagram of placemat showing how to begin the design layout. The main motif is glued to the centre front and the other motifs are arranged up the sides towards the top corners.

been missed. More than likely it will be the reaction of the crackle on the blue paint.

6. Leave for at least twelve hours to dry. The crackling process will continue for an hour or more once it has begun allowing the gold undercoat to show through.

7. Carefully cut out all the fine paper images, making sure that all background or white paper has been removed. When the mats are dry, arrange the paper cut-outs in a pleasing design.

8. In this instance the acrylic sealer or Liquitex is also the glue. Brush the sealer onto the back of each motif and glue it in place on the crackled surface, using tweezers if necessary to move small pieces into position. Begin from the centre of the bottom edge and work upwards towards the top corners (Fig. 9).

9. Brush the sealer or Liquitex varnish over the surface of the placemat or coaster, gently brushing out any air bubbles. Leave for two or three hours to dry.

10. Apply two more coats of the sealer, leaving it to dry thoroughly between coats. Once this has dried completely, apply ten coats of clear gloss enamel, leaving at least twelve hours drying time between each one.

11. You can either leave the mats with the full gloss finish or lightly sandpaper the tops before polishing with a beeswax or silicone polish.

12. Complete the napkin rings in the same manner.

Australian parrots placemats and coasters

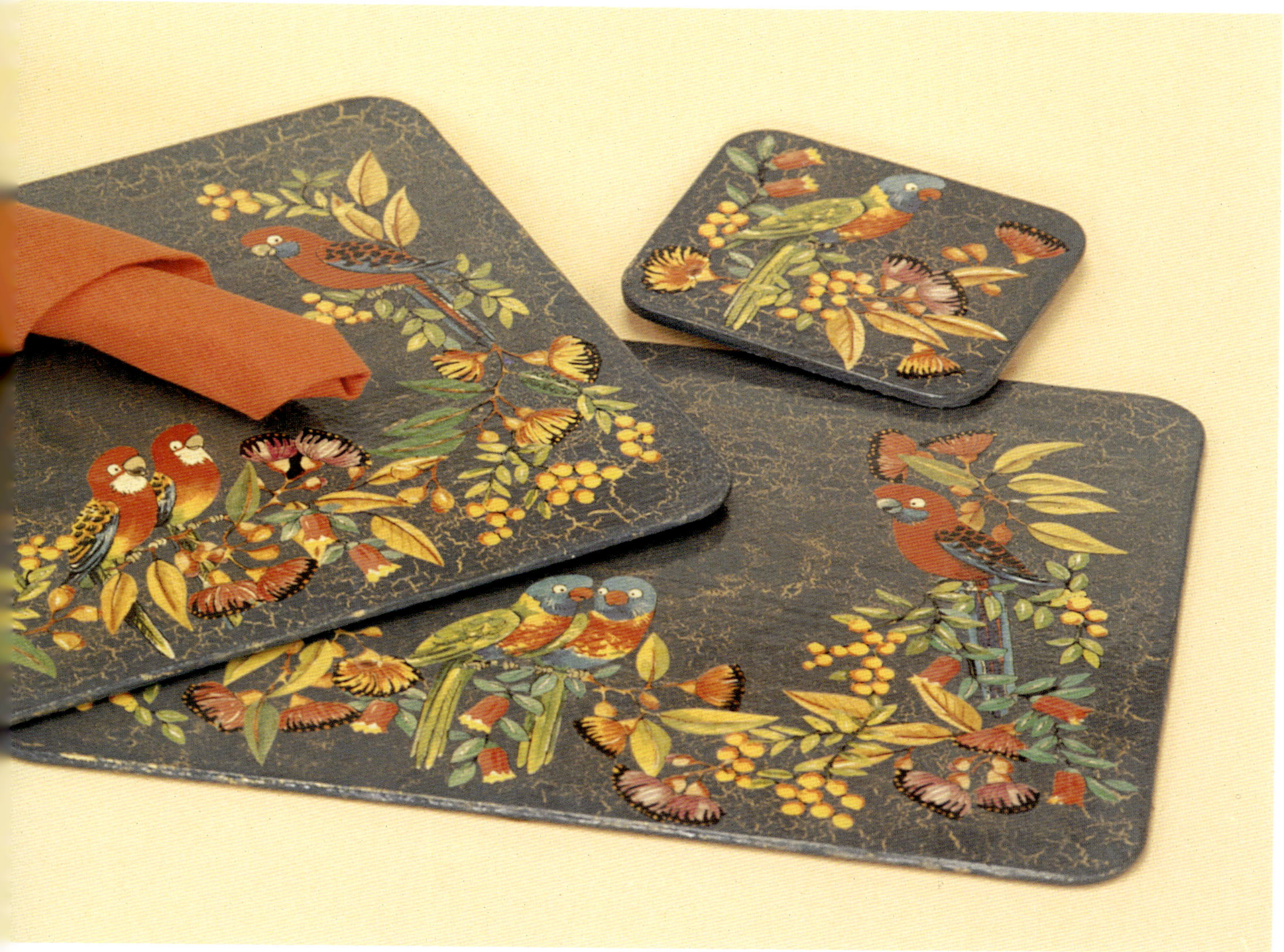

Photo album cover (page 36)

34

35

Papier-mâché boxes

flower stamps with the wildflower paper or the koala stamps to match the design of koalas and flowers.

7. Evenly dab the stamp onto the embossing liquid stamp pad and, with one hand inside the box to support the area being stamped, press the stamp firmly onto the outside. Sprinkle a generous amount of the gold embossing glitter over the clear stamped design then tip the excess glitter onto a piece of paper. Use a soft brush to remove any small flecks of gold which have stuck to the box outside the design area.

8. Hold the box, design side down, over a source of heat (I used a toaster) until the embossing fluid and heat react to melt the gold glitter into a solid gold outline. Watch carefully as this process takes only a few seconds. Repeat the process, one side at a time, until all six sides of the box have been embossed.

Note If one of the stamped sides does not work on the first attempt, with the embossing appearing blotchy or smudged, simply wait until the stamp is perfectly dry and paint over that section of the box with the black acrylic paint. Leave for an hour or two while the paint dries, then try again.

Greeting cards and bookmarks

Sample pictures Butterflies from Mamelok Press Scrap Sheet No. 811 (see Supplier's List at the back of this book). Gum blossom and gum leaf motifs from Koalas in Wildflowers from Phil Taylor Studios. Assorted pictures of landscapes and wildflowers from books, cards and travel brochures.

Individual handmade greetings cards and bookmarks made from blanks and trimmed with pictures, photographs, ribbons and laces, pressed flowers, cross-stitched embroidery and paper quilling can be a tremendous source of satisfaction to the creator as well as provide immense pleasure to the recipient. These samples of handmade original cards have a picture or motif in the central aperture with a variety of paper cut-outs and paper-tole flowers and butterflies around the edges. Others have a gold embossed stamp on the outside with the three-dimensional effect in the centre.

Materials
Cards and bookmark blanks available from Swanland Crafts in Western Australia in packs of five (see Supplier's List at the back of this book)
Suitable pictures or photographs to fill the oval or long aperture
Small paper cut-outs to trim the corners and for use in the paper-tole projects
Craft glue
Small scissors with sharp-pointed blades
Acrylic sealer such as Liquitex gloss medium
Tube of Silicone clear household seal and glue

Directions
1. Open the three-fold card or bookmark until it is flat. Apply a thin line of the craft glue around the edge of the aperture on the wrong side and lay the card, right side up, glue side down, onto the picture or photograph so that it is framed in the opening.
2. Once the glue has dried, fold the left-hand flap over the back of the picture and glue into position by running a fine line of craft glue around all three sides of the flap before pressing it down (Fig. 12).
3. Cut out two or three copies of each motif which needs to be glued to the outside of the aperture to form the paper-tole corners, making sure that every tiny piece of background paper has been removed from each.

fold left-hand flap over centre panel

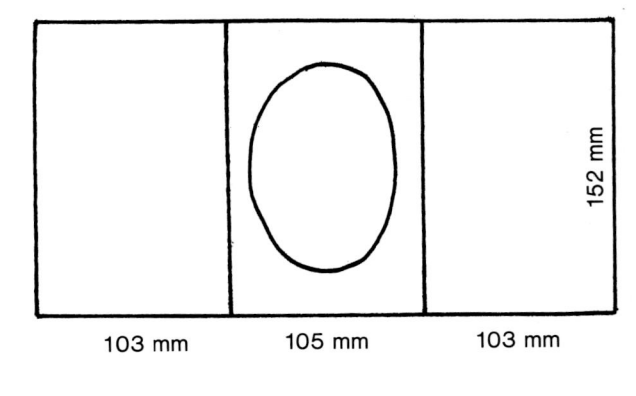

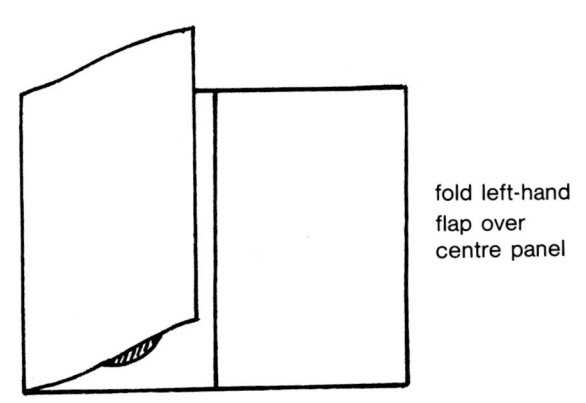

Fig. 12. Measurements for cutting out a three-fold card and diagram showing how to fold the left-hand panel over the back of oval aperture in the centre panel.

Greeting cards and bookmarks

4. Using the craft glue, stick the first motif to the card corner, applying the glue to the centre of the back of the motif.

5. Gently raise the edges of the corner motif and coat with a layer of the acrylic sealer. When this has dried, squeeze a small dob of the silicone clear household sealer and glue to the centre of the motif and place the next identical motif onto the rubbery glue. Once again lift the edges by curling them slightly over a pencil and coat with the acrylic gloss sealer (Fig. 13).

6. Repeat this process, adding layers of leaves and flowers as required. Arrange the wings of the butterflies into a natural position before adding a final coat of the acrylic gloss sealer.

7. Alternatively, use a rubber stamp with a corner motif (obtainable from Craft Impressions in Western Australia) and press it into an embossing fluid stamp pad. Press the stamp firmly onto the corners of the card and spread over a thick layer of gold embossing glitter. Hold the card face down over the heat of a toaster until the fluid and glitter melt into a solid gold line.

8. Glue a coloured picture or photograph behind the oval aperture and glue the card together by folding the left-hand flap over the back of the picture.

9. For the bookmarks, glue the background scenery behind the long aperture. Fold the left-hand flap over this and glue into position. On the front of the bookmark glue a second motif such as a kangaroo or koala, then glue the final layer of leaves, grass or flowers over the bottom edge of this second motif.

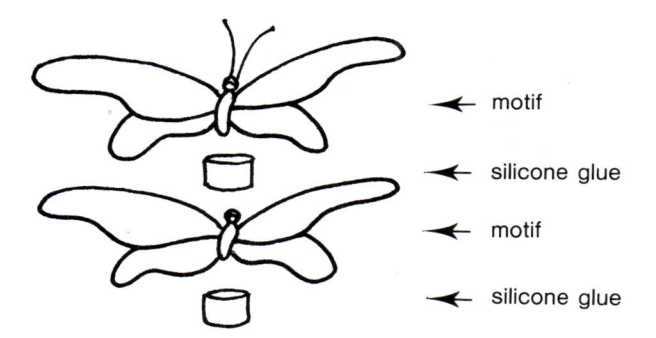

Fig. 13. Glue the first butterfly or flower motif to the card with a small dab of the silicone glue. Squeeze a second small dab of the glue on the centre of the previous motif and place the second identical motif on the top. With a pencil, slightly curve the wings or petals to form a realistic shape.

Christmas decorations

Sample paper Poinsettias by Card Sharp.

For those who prefer home-crafted Christmas decorations, these made from polystyrene shapes are bright, colourful and very Australian, with the use of poinsettia paper cut-outs and a gumnut trimming. The same idea could be readily adapted to Victorian-style decorations by painting the shapes black or burgundy, adding suitable period paper motifs and a gold lace trim.

Materials
Polystyrene balls or eggs
Colourful Christmas paper
Gold acrylic paint
Liquitex acrylic varnish
Assorted small gumnuts
Gold braid, measured around the shape for size
Craft glue and wooden satay sticks
25 cm gold cord
Small length (approximately 10 cm) fine wire
Clear gloss enamel such as Estapol or MonoCel
Acrylic paint for undercoat
Block of styrofoam packaging

Directions
1. To make the polystyrene shapes easier to handle while painting, push the pointed end of a satay stick into them at the seam at the bottom.
2. The sticks can then be pushed into a larger piece of styrofoam while the paint dries.
3. Cover each shape with the undercoat and leave for at least two hours. If necessary add a second coat.
4. Once the undercoat is thoroughly dry, cover with two coats of gold acrylic, leaving two or three hours drying time between them. Leave the satay sticks in place.
5. Carefully cut out the paper images to be used on the decorations with small sharp-pointed scissors. Now cut snips around the complete paper shape, leaving only the area in the centre intact. This will allow the paper motif's edges to overlap one another and follow the rounded shape of the ball or egg (Fig. 14).
6. Glue the paper cut-outs onto the ball using the Liquitex sealer or varnish as the glue. On the balls I used a lot of motifs to almost cover the surface, while on the eggs I glued a single picture on each side. This is strictly a personal choice but it is more interesting to vary the designs.
7. Gently rub each motif with the fingertips as it is glued into position, firstly to remove all excess glue and air bubbles and secondly to make sure that all the snipped edges are overlapped evenly and secured.

Fig. 14. Motif for the Christmas decoration with heavy lines showing where to snip the edges so that they will overlap. The arrow points to a common fault with snipping: Avoid finishing two snips in the same place because the paper between the snips will fall off altogether.

Poinsettia Christmas decorations

8. Now comes the fun part! Open your tin of clear gloss enamel and dunk the decoration in, covering the entire shape. Hold over the tin for a few seconds to drain off the excess varnish, then stand the satay stick in the block of styrofoam packaging again while the varnish drains and the decoration dries.
9. If the polystyrene shape is to be trimmed with gold braid pin one end of the braid to the centre of the bottom and then run a thin line of craft glue around the shape. Quickly follow the glue line with the braid, pressing it firmly to the seam line. Once the braid is glued into position, pin the other end flush with the first one. Trim off any excess braid as the two ends do not need to overlap (Fig. 15).
10. With the satay stick still positioned in the styrofoam packaging, squeeze a generous blob of clear-drying silicone sealer onto the bottom of the decoration. Arrange the gumnuts closely together in this glue and remove the stick from the decoration. Hold the decoration in your hand, upside-down, until the glue begins to dry, pushing the nuts together if they begin to slip apart.
11. Once the glue is holding the gumnuts firmly, you can rest the shape against a prop until the trimming is thoroughly dry.
12. Paint the nuts with the gold acrylic paint and leave for two or three hours to dry. Coat with the Liquitex acrylic sealer and leave for another two hours. Finally varnish them with the clear gloss enamel and leave overnight while they dry properly.
13. Bend the wire over a pencil to achieve a rounded shape. Glue both ends of the wire and push them into the top of the decoration. Thread the gold cord through the wire loop and tie the ends to form the hanger.

Fig. 15. Christmas decoration showing the positions of the pins to hold the ends of the gold braid and the wire loop at the top. Dip the ends in glue before pushing them into the polystyrene shape.

Kerosene lamp

Sample paper Australian Animals by Evelyn Studios, code numbers BW13 and BW14.

The humble kerosene lamp has become quite a collectable item now that we are enjoying the privileges of the modern era. Over the years kerosene lamps have come in many different shapes and sizes and are now regarded as valuable antiques. Modern versions readily available from camping stores and Army Surplus shops are suitable

Kerosene lamp

for decorating with découpage, folk art painting and stippling, creating a completely new range of craft collectables.

Materials
Modern kerosene lamp
Acrylic base-coloured paint, preferably black
Craft glue
Acrylic sealer such as Liquitex
Clear gloss enamel such as Estapol
Paper cut-outs small enough to fit around the lamp base and top
Stickytape
Small sharp-pointed scissors and soft-bristled paint brush

Directions
1. Lay the stickytape on the glass chimney under the wire supports to protect the glass from paint marks.
2. Carefully paint the lamp base, wire supports and handle with the base-coloured paint. Leave for at least three hours to dry thoroughly between coats and apply two more coats.
3. Carefully cut out enough small motifs to glue around the lampbase and top. Remove any pieces of background. This can be fiddly but the end result is well worth the effort involved.
4. Using the craft glue sparingly, evenly space the paper cut-outs around the lamp. When the glue has dried completely, apply two coats of the acrylic sealer. Leave for at least two hours.
5. Paint two coats of the clear gloss enamel over the lamp, making sure no areas have been missed, particularly under the top. Leave overnight between coats.
6. When the enamel has dried, peel away the stickytape from the glass under the crossed wire supports and clean off any small spots of dried paint with a scalpel.

Aussie mixture bookends

Sample paper Wildflowers and birds in stained glass paper from Aqua Unicorn Images Pty Ltd and a mixture of Australian style cut-outs from travel brochures, books and cards.

These bookends, bought for a few cents from a flea market, were initially painted pale pink. I liked the size and shape of them and could see that their solid appearance would certainly lend itself to

Aussie mixture bookends

découpage. They were constructed very simply from two pieces of wood, one piece measuring 15 cm × 12 cm × 2 cm and the other 12 cm × 10 cm × 2 cm.

Materials
2 pieces of timber 15 cm × 12 cm × 2 cm
2 pieces of timber 12 cm × 10 cm × 2 cm
Several different paper motifs cut from various sources (cut more than you will need to give yourself enough individual motifs to overlap and fill in all the background areas)
A mixture of three parts Clag and one part PVA glue
Acrylic sealer such as Liquitex
Two 12 cm squares of felt
Woodworking glue
Clear gloss enamel
Selleys Polyglaze Cut and Polish
Polish such as Silicone Glaze

Directions
1. Glue the bookends together as shown in Fig. 16, using the PVA woodworking glue. Support the bookends until the glue has dried completely.
2. Round off the four outer corners with a small piece of fine sandpaper and sand off any rough areas on the bookends themselves.
3. Leaving the bottom free, cover the sides and the back with pictures, overlapping them around the narrow edges of the back and base. Make sure that there are no spaces left uncovered, overlapping pictures and trimming the corners. Leave the best pictures for the front.
4. Totally cover the pictures on the front, back, base and edges with two coats of the acrylic sealer, leaving at least three hours of drying time in between coats.
5. Cover picture surfaces with approximately twenty coats of the clear gloss enamel, leaving at least twelve hours of drying time between each one, preferably overnight.
6. When enough coats of varnish have been applied to sink the pictures, gently rub on the Selleys Cut and Polish until the shine has been removed.
7. Polish to a mellow shine with the Silicone Glaze.
8. Spread an even coating of clear-drying PVA glue over the bottom of each bookend and carefully smooth on the felt pieces with the fingers, pushing any wrinkles or bubbles to the outer edges. Leave overnight to dry.

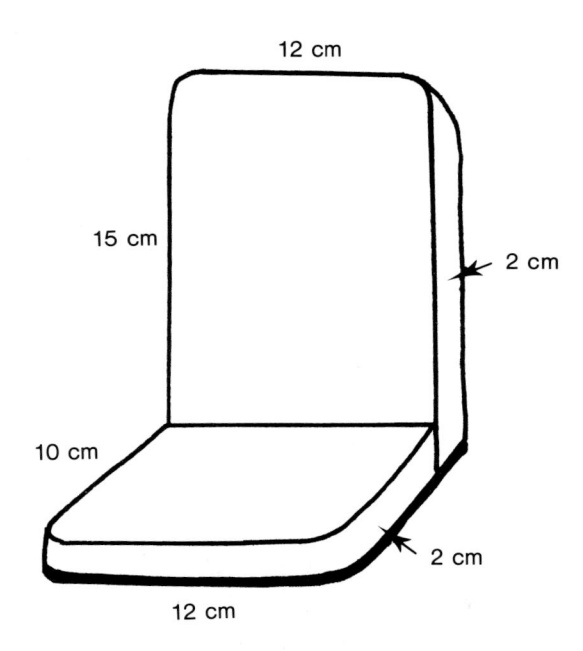

Fig. 16. Measurements and construction of the bookends

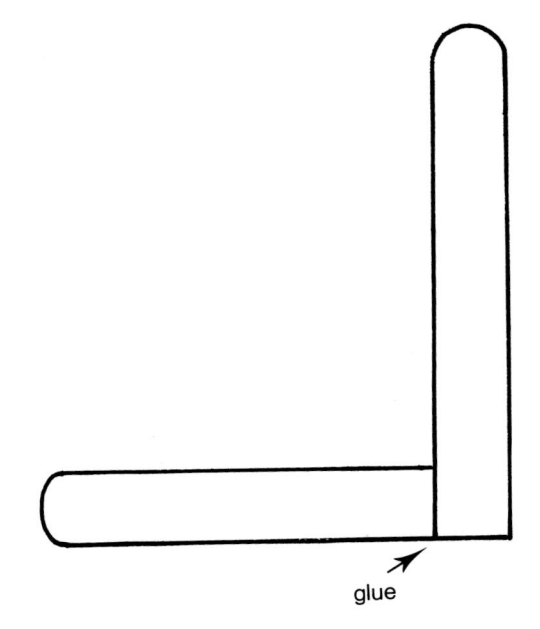

Doll's wardrobe and cot

Sample paper Ballerina Koalas from Evelyn Studios, code No. BW15.

Doll's furniture such as this wardrobe and the rocking cot do not have to be solely for little girls to play with. This particular set of furniture had been quietly relegated to the shed about twelve years ago once my own two little girls had grown too old for such childish pursuits. Thankfully, I could never bring myself to part with them, even though the girls had absolutely no sentimental attachment to them, and when I was looking around for projects to découpage both pieces of furniture showed a lot of potential. Now I find that

Doll's furniture

suddenly I have two very big girls who want their shared furniture back to display various collections of teddy bears and old dolls!

Materials

Wooden furniture such as the dolls' furniture in the project: chairs, small tables, stools and chests of drawers
Suitable childish pictures cut from wrapping paper, greetings cards and calendars
Craft glue
Small tin of undercoat
Small tin of flat enamel paint in pastel colour
Sandpaper
Acrylic sealer
Small sharp scissors and a soft-bristled brush

Directions

1. Sandpaper the surface of the object to remove all flakes of old paint, splinters and rough areas. Wipe off the dust with a clean soft cloth.
2. Cover the furniture with the undercoat so that all areas are sealed. If the furniture, like mine, is several years old, the wood may be dry and the first coat of undercoat will soak straight in. Two or three applications of undercoat may be required before the wood is ready for the final coat of paint.
3. Apply two layers of pastel coloured paint, leaving overnight to dry completely between coats.
4. Cut out the paper motifs carefully using the fine-pointed scissors, making sure that every tiny piece of background paper has been removed.
5. Using the soft brush, paint each picture on the back and the front with the acrylic sealer and varnish. This will prevent the ink in the paper absorbing the clear gloss enamel when it is applied or leaking out and running into other colours.
6. Arrange the pictures onto the doors and other solid areas so that they form an attractive and coordinating design. It may be helpful at this stage to secure each picture with a little piece of Blu-tack.
7. Smear the craft glue or a mixture of one part Clag and two parts PVA woodworking glue onto the back of each paper cut-out and glue into position. Allow several hours, preferably overnight, to dry.
8. Cover the pictures only (not the woodwork) with a final layer of acrylic seal and varnish such as Liquitex.

Ballerina koalas box

Sample paper Ballerina Koalas from Evelyn Studios, code No. BW15.

For all little girls who love ballet, koalas and boxes in which to keep treasures, this box is guaranteed to win hearts. The background surface can be painted to match any decor, while the koalas wear an assortment of coloured bodices with snowy white tutus. Alternatively, the box could be covered with pictures cut from wrapping paper or books to blend with any particular theme, such as a particular sport, pop group, pets or hobby.

Materials
Large papier-mâché box with a lid
Acrylic paint for background colour
Gold acrylic paint for stippling
Gold lace to fit around the bottom edge of the lid with a 1 cm overlap
7 mm wide satin ribbon to fit around the top of the lace (plus 20 cm extra for a bow if desired)
Craft glue
Acrylic sealer such as Liquitex
Small piece of fine kitchen sponge
Soft cloth to wipe out air bubbles and wrinkles
Small sharp-pointed scissors
Paper cut-outs for the top and sides of the box

Directions
1. Apply three coats of the base-coloured acrylic paint to the box and the lid, leaving at least two to three hours of drying time between each one.
2. Spread a little of the gold acrylic paint onto the sponge, dabbing the excess gold onto a piece of scrap paper. When the sponge is almost dry and the gold specks are small and separated, quickly and firmly dab the sponge over the box to cover as large an area as possible. Renew the gold paint on the sponge as necessary, always wiping the excess paint onto the paper first.
3. Allow the gold stippled surface at least two hours to dry completely. Meanwhile carefully cut out

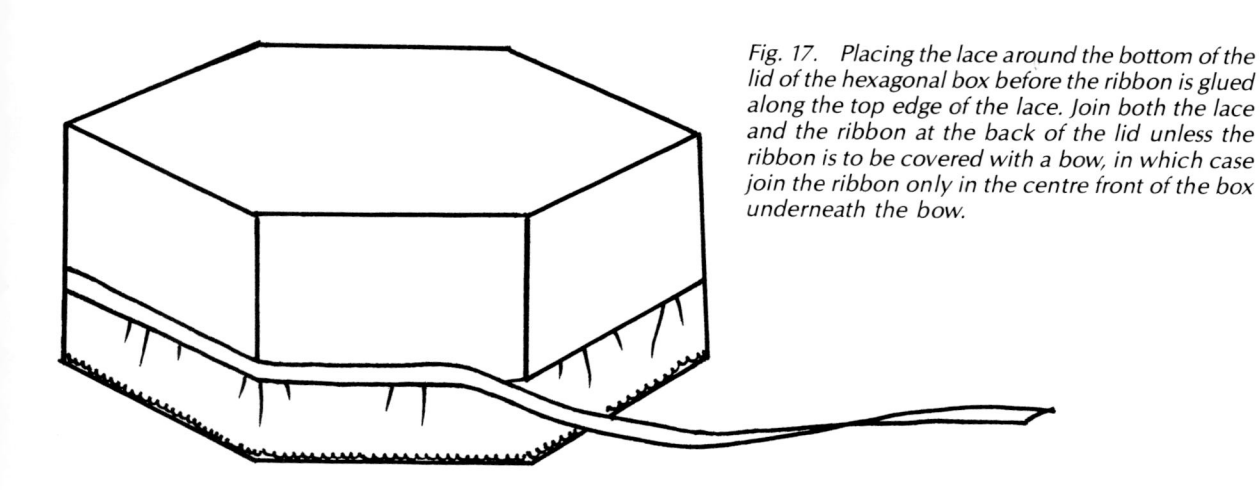

Fig. 17. Placing the lace around the bottom of the lid of the hexagonal box before the ribbon is glued along the top edge of the lace. Join both the lace and the ribbon at the back of the lid unless the ribbon is to be covered with a bow, in which case join the ribbon only in the centre front of the box underneath the bow.

Ballerina koalas papier-mâché box

enough pictures to arrange on the top and sides of the lid and the sides of the box.

4. Using craft glue, stick the motifs to the top and sides of the lid, leaving room around the bottom edge of the lid for the lace trimming and the ribbon.

5. Replace the lid on the box and mark very lightly where the bottom edge reaches down the sides of the box. Do not glue any pictures above this line.

6. Glue paper cut-outs around the box, centring them on each of the six sides.

7. Once the glue has dried completely, apply three coats of the acrylic gloss sealer, leaving at least two or three hours between each application.

8. Glue the lace around the lid, keeping the bottom edge of both the box lid and the lace together. Overlap the two ends at the back of the box lid and glue neatly.

9. Glue the satin ribbon around the top of the lace, once again overlapping the joining ends and gluing together. Make a small bow if desired and glue into place on the ribbon at the front of the lid (Fig. 17 on page 51).

Wooden magazine rack

Wooden magazine rack

Sample papers Weeping Bottlebrush paper from Pettis Studios and scenic landscapes from a calendar or book. The magazine holder is from Timber Turn.

Rather than paint the magazine holder before glueing the pictures onto the front and back I decided to leave the natural timber look. There are several really interesting wooden items available on the market at the moment which are suitable for both découpage and folk art painting and all of them could be treated in much the same way.

Materials
Wooden magazine holder
Large pictures cut from a pictorial calendar or book
Mixture of 3 parts Clag and 1 part PVA wood-
    working glue
Acrylic sealer and varnish
Wrapping paper or cards with wildflower designs
Small sharp-pointed scissors
Sandpaper
Clear gloss enamel

Directions
1. Sandpaper the entire surface of the wooden item, including all the edges. Wipe away all excess dust with a soft clean cloth.
2. Cut out the large landscape pictures and apply the acrylic sealer to both sides. Leave for at least three hours to dry thoroughly.
3. Glue these pictures on the centre back and centre front before arranging the wildflowers around the edges (Fig. 18). Glue everything in position carefully wiping away any excess glue and squeezing out all air bubbles.
4. Once the glue has dried, apply a coat of acrylic sealer to the pictures to prevent any leaks of the gloss enamel onto the paper.
5. Apply three coats of the gloss enamel to the magazine holder both inside and out, leaving overnight between coats.

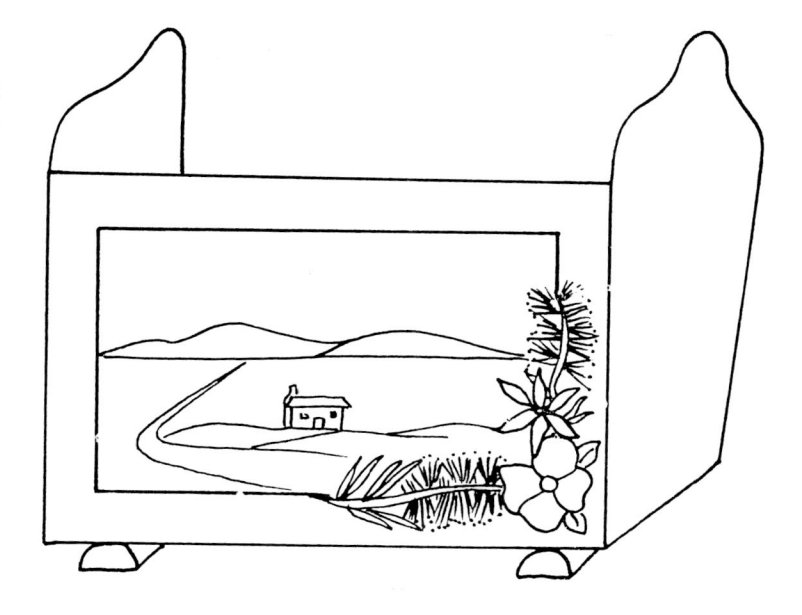

Fig. 18. Glue the large landscape pictures to the front and back of the magazine holder, then cover the straight edges with smaller cut-outs of wildflowers or birds.

Goldfields letterbox

Sample paper Pictures cut from colourful travel brochures.

What better way to tell the world where your heart belongs than to découpage a letterbox with pictures or photographs of a particular area? Not only will you have the most colourful letterbox in the street, you will also have the most interesting! It is amazing just how many people have recognised the pictures on this letterbox as being representative of the Kalgoorlie-Boulder goldfields area and have stopped to tell me how much they also love the place. Perhaps the letterbox of your choice could be découpaged with images from another country or state, pictures of wildflowers and birds or with an old-fashioned Victorian theme—the choice is only as limited as imagination will allow!

Materials
Commercial letterbox with a flat front panel suitable for découpage
Outdoor flat paint used for pergolas and gutters
Clear gloss enamel
Acrylic sealer such as Liquitex
Travel brochures with a theme or other suitable pictures
Small sharp-pointed scissors
Craft glue or a mixture of 3 parts Clag with 1 part PVA
Sandpaper

Directions
1. Sandpaper the letterbox and the post until both are free from splinters and rough areas.
2. Paint both pieces with as many coats of paint as are needed to completely cover the wooden surface. The sample letterbox required four coats of paint, left overnight to dry between each.
3. Carefully cut out the pictures, making sure that every tiny piece of background paper has been removed. Choose two or three larger pictures to form the background with smaller pictures to be glued across the front of these.
4. Cover all of these pictures on both sides with a coat of the acrylic sealer or varnish to prevent the gloss enamel seeping into the paper.

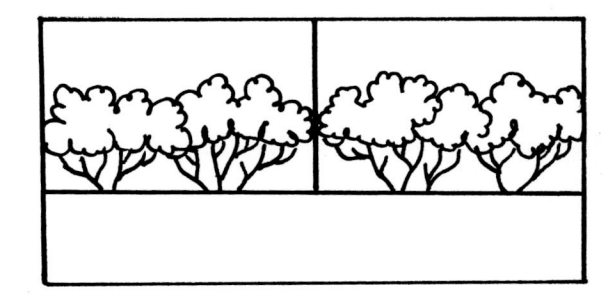

Fig. 19. Glue a large background picture or two pieces of background onto the front of the box first. Glue cut-outs over the join if you have two pictures meeting at the centre of the front panel. Glue smaller motifs along the bottom of the panel, covering the bottom of the background pictures.

Goldfields letterbox

5. Glue the background pictures onto the front of the letterbox first, carefully removing any air bubbles with a soft clean cloth. Once the glue has dried properly, overlap the smaller pictures on top (Fig. 19).
6. Cover the découpaged front panel with a coat of the acrylic sealer and leave for two hours to dry.
7. Varnish the entire front of the letterbox with two or three coats of clear gloss enamel, leaving it for at least twelve hours overnight to dry between coats.
8. Secure the post in the ground before attaching the letterbox to the top with nails or screws. Screw the house numbers to the post where they can be clearly seen.

Miniatures in a shadow box

Thimble

Materials
China thimble from a souvenir shop
Tiny paper cut-outs from travel brochures and scrapbook picture sheets
Craft glue
Acrylic sealer
Clear gloss enamel
Acrylic paint

Directions
1. Paint the thimble both inside and out with two coats of the acrylic paint, leaving at least two hours to dry between coats.
2. Glue the pictures in a design on the front of the thimble.
3. Cover with two coats of the acrylic sealer.
4. Apply two further coats of the clear gloss enamel.
5. When this is thoroughly dry, apply a small paper cut-out such as a butterfly or flower to the top of the thimble, folding the wings or petals so that they stand up from the china.
6. When the glue has dried, paint the motif with a coat of the clear gloss enamel.

Wooden vase and bowl

Materials
Small wooden items from a doll's house supplier
Tiny paper cut-outs from wrapping paper and brochures
Craft glue
Acrylic base paint
Clear gloss enamel
Acrylic sealer

Directions
1. Paint the wooden item with the acrylic base paint. If required, apply a second coat once the first one has had two hours drying time.
2. Glue the pictures to the front of the bowl and all over the vase, overlapping them so that no background paint remains to be seen.
3. Cover the bowl or vase with the acrylic sealer to prevent the varnish leaking into the paper.
4. Once this has dried thoroughly, apply two coats of the clear gloss enamel, leaving overnight between coats.

Painting in a gold frame

Materials
Gold brooch back available from lapidary shops or craft shops
Picture cut from a travel brochure or book which will fit into the centre of the frame
Craft glue
Acrylic sealer
Varnish such as Estapol or MonoCel
Small picture stand available from a doll's house supplier

Directions
1. Cut out the small picture to fit the frame and paint it on both sides with the acrylic sealer.
2. Glue the picture into the centre of the brooch back frame. Use the point of a satay stick or nail file to press the edges flat.
3. Once the glue is dry, cover the entire picture and metal frame with a coat of clear gloss varnish.
4. Glue the framed picture onto the picture stand with the craft glue.

Miniatures in a shadow box

Gold and sepia toned plate

Materials
Pewter plate from a doll's house supplier
Gold acrylic paint
Acrylic sealer
Sepia picture cut from a diary or book
Clear gloss enamel

Directions
1. Paint the plate with the gold paint and leave to dry for at least two hours before applying a second coat and leaving to dry again.
2. Cut out the picture to fit exactly into the centre of the plate; coat both sides of the paper image with the acrylic sealer to prevent the varnish seeping into the paper.
3. Glue the picture into the centre of the plate. Once the glue has dried, cover the plate on both sides with two coats of the clear gloss enamel.

Photo frame

Small brass photo frame
Tiny paper cut-outs to fit into the corners of the frame
Acrylic sealer
Clear gloss enamel
Acrylic base paint
Photo to fit into the frame
Craft glue

Directions
1. Apply two or three coats of the acrylic base paint to evenly cover the brass. Allow up to two hours drying time between each coat of paint.
2. Cut out the corner motifs and cover each one, both front and back, with a coat of the acrylic sealer.
3. Glue the pictures into position.
4. Cover the frame front with a coat of the clear gloss enamel. When this has dried completely assemble the frame, glueing the photograph into position.

Pottery vase

This pottery vase can be decorated using the instructions given for the wooden vase but with the motifs being glued to the front only, in a similar manner to the wooden bowl.

Sepia-toned case

Sepia-toned facsimile pictures are available in calendars, old encyclopaedias, art prints, pictorial diaries and books. The sample pictures were used from the Angus & Robertson Australian Heritage Diary from 1993 with the kind permission of the publisher Allan Cornwell.

The wooden case was another gem discovered at a local swap-meet and costing just a few dollars. Several coats of varnish had to be removed with sandpaper before the sepia pictures could be glued onto the surface. When the case was completely covered with the sepia-toned pictures I found that it looked rather 'dead', and livened it up with one or two coloured pictures that were very subtle, the colours merging with the sepia tones rather than overpowering them.

Materials
Wooden or papier-mâché case or large box
Mixture of 3 parts Clag and 1 part PVA glue
Pictures in sepia tones to cover the entire surface
A few pictures in very subtle colours
Small sharp-pointed scissors
Acrylic sealer such as Liquitex
Clear gloss enamel such as Estapol or MonoCel
Sandpaper
Acrylic paint in brown
Rust treatment paint if hinges and catches are rusty

Directions
1. Sandpaper the surface of the case (if it is a wooden one) until the entire area is smooth. If the hinges and catches are showing signs of rust, rub them down with a small piece of steel wool to remove any excess dust and paint. Wipe with a clean cloth to remove the residue and treat with a rust-killing paint available from hardware stores.
2. Where the hinges and corner protectors have been screwed onto the case, take them off and store them in a glass jar; this will make the positioning of the pictures easier. If the handles and catches have been rivetted in place, the pictures will have to be carefully cut around them.
3. Cut out the sepia-toned paper images from as many sources as you need until you have enough to cover the back, front and sides of the case and lid. The paper from calendars and pictorial diaries is usually very porous and literally drinks in varnish, so it is absolutely imperative that each picture be coated with two coats of acrylic gloss sealer (including the edges).
4. Cut out the softly coloured pictures and seal these as well to prevent their colours leaking out or the paper soaking in the clear gloss enamel. Be very particular about removing every tiny scrap of white background paper as this will show up quite vividly against all the sepia and cream tones.
5. Cover the sanded surface with a coat of acrylic undercoat. This gives a flat base to aid glue adhesion. Begin at the centre of the lid and glue on any main pictures. Gradually work out to the sides, overlapping the pictures and avoiding any perfectly straight edges. Smooth the glue onto the backs of the pictures with the fingers. When each motif has been securely stuck, push out any excess glue and air bubbles with a small roller or soft cloth.
6. Take the pictures over the corners by glueing the main part of the motif onto the case and leaving the rest of it hanging out over the edge. Fold the picture over the side of the case and press it down the other way, once again with the excess area of motif hanging over the edge. Pinch the two sides of the spare paper which is over the edge together and cut off the triangle level with and close to the corner.
7. Leave each area of the case to dry for at least

Sepia-toned case

twelve hours before coating with another coat of acrylic sealer.

8. Paint all the metal hinges, catches, handles and corners with a dark brown acrylic paint. If these have been removed first, paint each individual screw and hinge, placing them carefully on a tray when finished so that they do not get lost while they are drying. If the metal attachments are fixed to the case with rivets, it may be easier to paint them before the pictures are glued into position.

9. Finish off the case with five coats of the clear gloss enamel, leaving overnight to dry between coats. Paint the screws, hinges, handles and catches with the gloss enamel while they are separated from the main body of the case.

10. Carefully replace all the bits and pieces with a small screwdriver when the case is completely dry.

Wattle tin tray

Sample paper   Pettis Studios Australian Wattles.

It seems such a waste when something like this old metal tray is going to be thrown out onto the rubbish tip, when with a coat of brightly coloured paint and some equally colourful pictures it can be transformed into an attractive and usable item. This particular tray had a rather worn advertising facsimile picture on the front, a scratched border and two small rust spots beginning to form on the lip. Obviously the rust needed to be treated first, so the surface was sandpapered back at the rust spots then painted with a rust-killing solution available from paint and hardware stores.

Materials
Metal tray (or a wooden tray if available)
Acrylic paint for the background
Acrylic sealer such as Liquitex
Suitable paper cut-outs
Small sharp-pointed scissors
Clear gloss enamel such as Estapol
Sandpaper or Selleys Cut and Polish
Beeswax polish or silicone glaze
A mixture of 3 parts Clag and 1 part PVA woodglue

Directions
1. Treat any rust spots in the metal with a rust-killing paint once the surface around the rust has been sanded smooth. Dut off any rust powder remaining.
2. Paint the tray with an undercoat of acrylic paint and leave for at least two hours to dry. The tray will probably require three or four coats of paint before it is completely covered, leaving for two hours between coats.
3. Once the paint is completely dry, cut out the paper images with the pointed scissors, making sure that every small piece of white or coloured background paper has been removed. While this will take time and patience the result will be well worth the effort.
4. Using the mixture of 3 parts Clag and 1 part PVA glue position the pictures around the tray. Any open areas can be filled in with smaller pictures glued over the top of the first layer.

Wattle tin tray

5. Completely cover the surface of the tray with a coating of acrylic sealer and varnish. Leave for two to three hours to dry.
6. Paint a coating of the clear gloss enamel on the tray, including the lip and over the edges, and leave overnight or at least for twelve hours to dry. Apply another twenty coats of clear gloss until the paper images are completely 'sunk', once again leaving twelve to twenty-four hours between coats.
7. Cut the surface back with either sandpaper or cut and polish, and buff up the dull surface with beeswax polish or silicone glaze.

Suppliers

Pettis Studios
78 Charles Street
Kew Vic. 3101

Phil Taylor Studios
Unit B1, 6 Durdans Avenue
Rosebery NSW 2018

Card Sharp
74 Old Barrenjoey Road
Avalon NSW 2107

Evelyn Studios
PO Box 261
Mt Evelyn Vic. 3796

Aqua Unicorn Images Pty Ltd
107 Ormond Rd,
Elwood Vic. 3184

Craft Impressions
(exclusive Australian-designed rubber stamps)
PO Box 195
Greenwood Western Australia 6024

Swanland Crafts
(card blanks and bookmarks)
PO Box 228
Belmont Western Australia 6104
(Pack of 5 pastel cards $6.50; pack of 5 black bookmarks $4.50; includes postage and handling.)

Timber Turn
1 Shepley Avenue
Panorama South Australia 5041

Rosenhain, Lipmann and Peers Pty Ltd
(for the butterfly scrap pictures)
147 Burnley St
Richmond Vic. 3121

Index

Acrylic paints, 7
Acrylic sealers, 8
Clear gloss enamels, 8
Cork placemats, preparation, 31
Crackling, 15
Crackling medium, 8
Doll's house miniatures, 58
Glues, 8

Pattern matching, 20
Paper motifs, source of, 10
Paper-tole, 41
Polystyrene shapes, 43
Sepia-toned pictures, 60
Stippling, 15
Three-fold cards, 40